Facing Two Sickles

Facing Two Sickles

Families Dealing with Sickle-Cell Disease

ZETTA SYLVIA BAILLOU-POITIER

FACING TWO SICKLES
FAMILIES DEALING WITH SICKLE-CELL DISEASE

Scripture quotations from the Holy Bible, King James Version (Authorized Version). First published in 1611. Quoted from the KJV Classic Reference Bible.

iUniverse books may be ordered through booksellers or by contacting:

iUniverse
1663 Liberty Drive
Bloomington, IN 47403
www.iuniverse.com
1-800-Authors (1-800-288-4677)

ISBN: 978-1-5320-7673-2 (sc)
ISBN: 978-1-5320-7674-9 (hc)
ISBN: 978-1-5320-7695-4 (e)

Library of Congress Control Number: 2019907703

Print information available on the last page.

iUniverse rev. date: 06/18/2019

CONTENTS

PREFACE

IN THE BIBLE, A SICKLE IS USED TO CUT EARS OF CORN NEAR
the top of their straw. Such a sickle is usually made
wholly of iron or steel and shaped much like the
instrument used in western lands. The smaller-sized
sickles are used for both pruning and reaping.

I imagine my children's sickle-cell disease (SCD)
doing something much like the sickle spoken of in
the Bible—the sickled red blood cells first block small
blood vessels and cut them down. And then they go
through a pruning and reaping season with painful
episodes while waiting to produce new or good red
blood cells. How can we not refer to the Bible when
the shape of the sickle used to cut the corn is the

same as that of the blood cells afflicted with sickle-cell disease?

Joel 3:13 (KJV) says, "Put ye in the sickle, for the harvest is ripe: come, get you down; for the press is full, the fats overflow; for their wickedness *is* great." This blood disorder is similar to the sickle because it presses you down, makes you tired, and makes you want to give up on life. Thank God for the words I deposited in my children's lives—to always trust Him, on good days and on bad days.

ACKNOWLEDGEMENTS

First, let me acknowledge the Holy Spirit, who has guided me from birth to this day. He has taught me to love God; my husband, Floyd; and my children despite the sickle challenge.

In addition, I acknowledge my parents, Horatio and Hazel Baillou, and Floyd's parents, Harold and Muriel Poitier (both deceased), who gave me all their support, as parents, to face the unknown despite the fact that our dealing with two children with the same disease was a first for both families.

To my other family members, friends, associates, and church family who have supported me in any way throughout this journey, thank you.

Furthermore, my sincere thanks to paediatrician

Paul Hunt and the staff at Sunrise Medical Centre and Miami Children's Hospital (now known as Nicklaus Children's Hospital) in South Florida for their love and support during our times in and out of the hospital.

To you, who I may have left out, thank you for taking the time to purchase this book or borrow it from a good friend to read.

May this book be an inspiration to you all.

INTRODUCTION

THIS BOOK IS DEDICATED TO AND HAS BEEN WRITTEN IN honour of my deceased daughter, Vashti Vernica Poitier (1990–2012), and my son, Vance Vasean Poitier.

In May 2010, my daughter, Vashti, aged twenty, said, "Mom, why don't we write a book on children suffering from sickle-cell disease and let people know what we, as a family, have gone through and that we are still standing." Since May 2010, I have been preparing to make this book a reality, in honour of both my children. On 18 July 2016, I began to transfer information onto a flash drive in an attempt to create this amazing book.

I also wrote this book to help encourage any parent or guardian who may be the caretaker of a child with sickle-cell disease. I want you to know that you are not alone out there. I feel your pain. As a matter of fact, I have felt and still feel your pain, twice!

CHAPTER 1
The Beginning of Our Journey

When I met my husband, Floyd Poitier, for me, it was love at first sight. I had no idea that he had the sickle-cell trait. He had no idea that I also had the sickle-cell trait. And he managed to sweep me off my feet just one month later, in April 1988.

We dated for eight months—yes, eight months. During that dating period, we knew that we were meant for each other. My mom and dad accepted him right away when they met him in May 1988. I think it was Mother's Day weekend that we travelled to Freeport, Grand Bahama, and he agreed to meet them.

Meeting a girl's parents is not easy, but he passed the test and got the thumbs up from the first meeting.

We were engaged that same year, on 10 December 1988, and married the following year on 2 December 1989 at the Zion Baptist Church in Freeport, Grand Bahama. During our engagement period, we learned our good habits and, of course, bad habits, along with getting to know each other's family better. And after our wedding, we honeymooned for one week in Santo Domingo, Dominican Republic. Oh, what an experience, with us never having spoken, learned, or known any Spanish, which is the main language there. We made it an awesome time, with great food and each other's company.

In our culture, it was not mandatory that people check for hereditary disease in each other's family before they got married. At the time, we had no idea what, if any, hereditary diseases existed within our families that may affect our children. Let me say this to people in love and considering marriage: it is a good idea to get a heredity test done before you say, "I do," just so you know what to expect.

If you are not yet in love, the results may determine whether you want to continue with the relationship. However, if you are in love or already married and the test proves positive for a hereditary disease, especially if the disease has no cure, you will have hard decisions to make, but I will advise that you trust God. Trust God in all situations in your relationship, and remember Proverbs 3:5 (KJV): "Trust in the Lord with all thine heart; and lean not unto thine own understanding."

Believe me when I say, "Trust God."

CHAPTER 2
The Decision to Start a Family

FLOYD AND I AGREED THAT WE BOTH WANTED CHILDREN and we would start extending our family early on in our marriage. This way, we could share our youth with them while it was on our side. Therefore, on our wedding night, the procedure started, and I dare not say what we did, because my parents will read this book. If you have parents who are eighty years old, out of respect, you dare not say such words around them.

We were thrilled when I discovered in December 1989 that we were going to have our first child and started getting ready for our new family right away.

For the first few months of my pregnancy, everything went as normal as any other pregnancy would.

At about six months, during a routine appointment, my doctor suggested that he test both Floyd and me to make sure we were not at risk of passing anything on to our child. As the doctor explained to us that the heredity test was a normal procedure, we thought, *Well, OK, why not? Let's go ahead and do it.*

When the doctor called us into the office to discuss the results, he told us something we never could have imagined in our wildest dreams. He informed us that we both had the sickle-cell trait and that it was very possible that our baby could have the disease.

Our first reaction was one of disbelief. Floyd and I had both heard about sickle-cell traits back in primary school, but we had never envisioned that, years later, it would actually make a difference in either of our lives. We had no idea that this blood disorder would have such a big impact in our world.

As I said, ladies, know your lifetime partner's family medical history. I recommend that you find this out, if possible, before marrying or while dating. Do not be afraid to ask, because I learned that this is just as important in a serious relationship as your financial standing.

Trust God; situations like this are what really put your faith to the test. Imagine going through with a pregnancy already knowing you were up against this. I did not change my mind about having children when we learned about the hereditary disease. I just stepped up my faith to another level. So, at that point, I rededicated my life to God and said, "God, this is in Your hands now. Whatever You do is well done." After that, I daily chanted, "Lord, whatever is Your will, that is what must be done, and not our will. I commit this matter entirely into Your hands."

The waiting—oh, the waiting! Psalm 27:14 (KJV) says, and I quote, "Wait on the Lord; be of good courage, and he shall strengthen thine heart; wait, I say, on the Lord!" Well, waiting with hopes of good news was the easy part. At the time, I read so many scriptures and religious materials that I felt like a walking book. I spent a freakish amount of time reading. When I look back on that behaviour now, I think God was only preparing me for this book.

CHAPTER 3
Learning about Sickle-Cell Disease

AFTER THAT LIFE-CHANGING APPOINTMENT, I STARTED reading every encyclopaedia I could find. Encyclopaedias are hardback books that sometimes have up to thirty-two volumes. They were very popular back in the '90s, especially if you did not have access to your own computer. I read them to see what I could learn about this thing called *sickle cell*, only to find over and over that this disease had no cure, only treatments. I read all the material I could get my hands on that had anything to do with any sort of blood disorder.

Sickle-cell disease (SCD), often called *sickle-cell*

anaemia or merely *sickle cell*, is an inherited condition that affects haemoglobin. Haemoglobin is a protein in the red blood cells that carries oxygen throughout the body. The red blood cells of someone with SCD look like sickles, or C-shaped tools, and that's where SCD gets its name. This abnormal haemoglobin is called *haemoglobin S* or *sickle haemoglobin.*

Because people with SCD have abnormal haemoglobin, their blood will not easily flow through the bloodstream. Their abnormally shaped red blood cells form rods that clump together, which causes the red blood cells to become rigid and curved. Consequently, these odd-shaped cells block blood flow. SCD is dangerous and can cause extreme pain, anaemia, and other symptoms.

According to the research Floyd and I found, SCD is the most common inherited blood disorder, meaning it is passed down through families. SCD is not contagious. People cannot catch or develop it later in life; only people born with it have it.

Carriers of the trait (such as Floyd and I) usually do not develop SCD symptoms, but unfortunately, they can pass the disease on to their children, especially if their partner also carries the sickle-cell trait. If both parents have the sickle-cell gene, then their child will usually have the severe type of this disorder. And if both parents carry the abnormal haemoglobin gene, it makes the possibility of their child's inheriting the disease even greater.

Between researching sickle cell and getting ready for the new baby, our lives were busy, nerve-racking, and stressful, but I still felt very blessed to be having my little girl. Since my pregnancy was as normal as any other, Floyd and I prayed for the best and that she would miraculously escape this disease.

I never could have imagined my child going through so much pain, and by this, I mean *really crazy pain*.

CHAPTER 4
The Birth of My First Child

I HAD NO MEDICAL ISSUES DURING MY PREGNANCY, ONLY the normal morning sickness and cravings. Finally, on 6 July 1990 at 5 p.m., my only sister, Izetta, took me to the hospital because I was having severe pains, and she said it may be time to give birth. With her experience, having gone through this four times, I concluded she had to be 100 per cent correct. I was so excited that I think my blood pressure went out of control right then.

When I went into labour, the medical team began to monitor my blood pressure right away. They asked me to please stay calm for the sake of my baby and told me they would do everything possible to reduce my blood pressure. I remained excited, which further elevated my blood pressure, and they informed me that they had to also monitor the baby's heartbeat.

Hours later, I heard the medical team say the baby's heart rate was decreasing and we may have to do an emergency caesarean delivery (surgical incision of the walls of the abdomen and uterus) to save both my life and my first offspring's life. The team needed my husband's approval for the surgery. Well, after the delivery, I was told that the baby's father had passed out and they had needed to monitor his blood pressure too. We experienced so much excitement before and during her arrival that my husband and I still joke about it today.

On 7 July 1990 at 7.59 p.m., I gave birth to our beautiful daughter, Vashti Vernica Poitier, at Rand Memorial Hospital in Freeport, Grand Bahama. From birth, we speculated that she may have SCD, because she had a very low birth weight for a nine-month baby, at 3 pounds 15.1 ounces. However, Floyd and I also assumed that by researching everything we could about the disease, we could protect her from having a crisis. Not so!

We could not have her tested for the disease until she was six months old; so we waited with bated breath and enjoyed our new baby daughter every single second. She was God's gift to us, and no matter what was inside her, we were going to fight it with everything we had.

When the time came for Vashti to be tested, we took her to a private clinic in Marsh Harbour, Abaco, where we lived. When she tested positive for sickle-cell disease, we decided that we would only have one child.

Vashti's fingers and toes slowly started to swell at around nine months old, and she would cry all night long. As a parent, you imagine that you would do anything to prevent your baby from getting hurt, but in reality, in situations like this, there is nothing— absolutely nothing—you can do to stop their pain. Some of the signs that we had read about were now a reality. We just had to give her some medication and wait for the pain to reduce.

At age one, Vashti spent her first severe pain crisis at Rand Memorial Hospital. The hospital's visiting hours did not allow Floyd and me to spend as much time with her as we wanted. Imagine leaving your baby with strangers and only being able to see her between 2 p.m. and 3 p.m. or 6 p.m. and 7 p.m. Wow, I tell you, waiting for visiting hours felt like years.

On our second visit, my husband asked the doctor if a private hospital had different visiting hours, because we wanted to sleep and spend more time with Vashti. When we discovered the private clinic did have different hours, we made arrangements with the private clinic, and she was relocated the next day. We were then able to spend more hours with her, which made us very comfortable.

Still, the doctors could only give her medication to reduce her pain; they couldn't make the disease go away. We had to come to terms with the fact that this was to become our daughter's way of life: doctor's visits, pain medications, and pills to take for life.

So, for the next couple of years, we battled with our baby daughter's sickle cell, and whenever she had a crisis, we gave her medication, and if it became worse, we would go to the clinic for further treatment. We did whatever was necessary to make her comfortable.

When she became able to talk, she would tell us where the pain was, and depending on its location, we would rub and kiss the area, which she said made her comfortable. It would take three to four days before we saw her feeling better.

Despite all of this, Vashti never let her sickness get in the way of her living and enjoying life. She said, "I do not want any of my friends feeling sorry for me."

As a child, Vashti was known as Miss Photogenic to everyone who knew her. Even as a toddler, she had to be the centre of attention. She would take photographs with anything, in any place, and with anyone she would find ready, willing, and able.

Vashti loved to dance and listen to music. She used to watch Barney videos over and over and could not get enough of *101 Dalmatians* and Winnie the Pooh. She was also very much into Barbie and Ken dolls. Her room was filled with the accessories, stuffed animals, books, videos, and anything else that resembled these so-called celebrities in her life.

In 1993, when she was three, Vashti started kindergarten at Vernita's Preschool in Dundas Town, Abaco. She graduated from her preschool as the head girl. She just loved school and making friends. Of course, she had to take many sick days, but she did not let that keep her spirits down. She could not wait to get back to school to see her friends and keep learning.

Once she started making friends, she always invited them over to the house; and before they went home, we had to make sure they ate, because she would not let them leave without breakfast, lunch, or dinner.

Vashti was such a joy to us in those first five years of her life. Even through the pain and medications and treatments, Floyd and I loved our precious little girl so very much. We took to heart every second with her because we knew we were not going to have any more children, as we did not wish for any other children of ours to suffer as Vashti did.

Many times, I wished I could take her place in the clinic and have those pains instead of her, seeing such a small child go through this and not able to play like she wanted to for fear that she would go into a painful crisis. I began to question God, *Why me?* But as I've looked back over the situation, I've realized it had to be me. I now believe that I was God's chosen vessel for such a time as that so I could encourage other families and especially inspire my own family.

I encouraged myself in the Lord and waited for my miracle.

CHAPTER 5
The Birth of My Second Child

However, once again, the Lord had other plans, and in June 1994, I found out that we were pregnant again!

I said to my husband, "OK, Floyd, we need to make a decision. If he has the disease, what do we do?" What were the odds of us having two children born with the disease when the encyclopaedia said that only one out of every four children would have the disease?

We did not have to wait long for an answer. During my seven month of pregnancy, I started having seizures. On 4 January, I became very sick and had a seizure, which the doctor said was due to my blood pressure suddenly elevating. The doctor advised me to go home and get some rest. However, later in the evening, I had a second seizure, and this time, the doctor instructed my husband to get me an emergency flight to the hospital in Nassau or Freeport.

Since most of our family members were in Freeport, he made the decision to transport me to Rand Memorial Hospital. Later, he told me we had a smooth flight with no seizure. Glory to God that I had no seizures on the plane, which we were advised may have impacted the baby's or my health.

We arrived safely on the ground in Grand Bahama; however, as soon as we landed, I am told that I had a seizure attack. The ambulance was waiting for us at the airport, and we were immediately transported to the hospital.

Once Floyd and I were at the hospital, I am told the staff examined me right away, and that is when the doctors told Floyd he needed to make a tough decision—save his baby or save his wife.

Floyd ultimately made the decision to save his wife; however, God intervened and gave him the both of us. On 5 January 1995, our son, Vance Poitier, was born at Rand Memorial Hospital in Freeport, Grand Bahama. His birth was also a caesarean delivery.

Two children delivered under the same conditions— two caesareans—and I am alive to tell the story. Thank You, Jesus! Trust God!

Vance was born prematurely and underweight, so he spent eight weeks in the hospital before he was released. Over this time, my faith in God continued to grow stronger, as I knew it was all in His hands.

During that time, I was told that on the way to the hospital for Vance's birth, my husband, in his haste to get me to Freeport, forgot to change his clothes. Remember, we lived in Abaco and had to get on the emergency flight to a hospital as soon as we could. Would you believe he went on the plane to Freeport in his boxers and a T-shirt?

Because he spent all day at the hospital in those clothes, other patients concluded that Floyd must have been a patient. It was not until 5 p.m. the evening of day of the birth —when other family members came to visit us and one of them asked him why he was still dressed in his boxers and T-shirt—that Floyd realized he had travelled like that the evening before and had not changed since we arrived at the hospital. He told the family member that only our safety, not how he was dressed, concerned him.

Thank you, Floyd. That was so sweet, but we still talk about it at family gatherings, and it is usually one of the biggest jokes on him.

Again, as with Vashti, Floyd and I had to wait six months after Vance was born before we could test him for sickle-cell disease. And again, as with Vashti, the test came back positive. So now we had two children with sickle-cell disease on our hands. We were overwhelmed. What would we do, or what would we continue to look out for?

We again scheduled a visit with Dr Hunt in Freeport to determine if Vance would receive the same medication that he would have given to Vashti. He took care of both our sick children and, when necessary, would refer them to Miami Children's Hospital in South Florida for further treatment.

Our life with Vance, as we remember it, was pills,

pills, and more pills. To see doctors, we travelled frequently to Miami for about six consecutive years. Vance had about twenty blood transfusions by the time he was eleven years old. Doctors told us to keep the blood transfusions going to exchange the bad cells for good cells. Then another doctor said to consider a bone marrow transplant, but we never took up that offer. I think the experience of trying everything and seeing that there really was no cure, but only medication for temporary relief, was the hardest part.

With Vance came the decision for me to undergo tubal ligation—or, as we say in the Bahamas, get my "tubes tied". Tubal ligation is a surgical procedure in which a woman's fallopian tubes are clamped, or blocked, and sealed. This is a permanent method of sterilization or birth control. It was a hard decision because I had wished to have more children, but due to Floyd's and my medical condition, doctors at that time said it was in our best interest to complete the procedure.

CHAPTER 6
Two Sickle Babies

By that time, Vashti was five, and she loved her baby brother very much. She was a great help to us, as she knew what he was going through and wanted to help him as much as possible. However, over the first two years of his life, Vance had more and more crises, many more than Vashti had when she was a baby and a toddler.

In 1997, when Vance was two years old, Floyd's mother moved to Freeport. We made the very difficult decision to let Vance move in with his grandmother, his aunt Mitchalean, and his aunt Raphaleta, now deceased, on the island of Freeport, as that allowed him to more quickly get to his doctor for pain medication. After all, Raphaleta was already his babysitter. Vance also spent time with his other aunts, Queenie and Izetta, on weekends to get to know these family members who also lived in Freeport.

When it came time for him to start kindergarten, we agreed that he would stay in Freeport, so Vance attended National Academy Kindergarten from three to five years of age. Deciding to have my baby grow up away from me was not easy, knowing that he was born premature and had sickle cell. *Not easy* is putting it mildly, but I managed to live with it because I knew one day he would get better.

Even though we missed him terribly, the years Vance lived in Freeport were a blessing, as Vance suffered many crises during his time in Freeport from age two to age fourteen. In September 2009, at age fourteen and a half, Vance moved back to Abaco for high school.

Floyd and I decided to give both our children the freedom to move between the two islands of Abaco and Freeport because our hospital in Abaco was not as well equipped as the hospital in Freeport. In a crisis, the home away from home was worth it, as that island afforded them better care. I can now picture Vashti and Vance trying to smile through all the pain so that family members would not see any hurt on their faces. The sad part is that we could do nothing else but immediately get them to a hospital for pain medication and in case they needed to be admitted.

Thank God for families. Our families, our friends, and especially our in-laws tremendously supported us, and there is no way we can thank them enough.

Let me pause here to say that if you love your spouse, then you should love and respect your in-laws. In our marriage, Floyd and I told each other from day one that we would never disrespect each other's families but love them all the same as our own. I am not saying our relationship was always 100 per cent and we always saw eye to eye. We had disagreements along the way, but with God's help, we stood by each other's families. Trust me, you can do it. Never give up on making amends, for trouble does not last always.

Forgiveness is not for the other person but for you— yes, you!

Vashti and Vance always got along very well whenever they were together. Even though they did not grow up together and lived on different islands, they spent their holidays and summers together and bonded as if they lived together, as I reminded them of each other and we made them talk daily on the phone. During their phone conversations, Vashti would usually encourage Vance to stay focused on his schoolwork, while Vance would tell Vashti to stop taking so many photos.

However, Vance did not call Floyd and me as often as we thought he should, because he did not like to talk on the telephone. So we would call him daily. Vance would mostly use his phone for schoolwork or to watch his favourite debates on YouTube. We had to beg him to please come to the phone just to say hello. Otherwise, he always just told Vashti, "Tell Mom and Dad I am OK." As his friends and family would say, he must really love you if you could get him on the phone for a conversation.

Memories are lasting, so let me encourage parents to keep memories alive. Spend quality time with your children, and cherish every minute you have with them. As a couple or a single parent, make sure you do things with your children, because you can never know what plans lie ahead for you; only God knows.

My two sick babies brought so much joy to our family that it has managed to keep us together. I know we kept some family members on their knees praying for us, and some awake drinking tea (from a can or from a bottle). But despite all of this, if you saw us at the hospital, you would not have known who the "in-laws" or "out-laws" were, because we had 100 per cent of their support. The Baillou and Poitier families truly are families to be reckoned with—we are strong, courageous, and loving people. And to think that all of this resulted from us, Floyd and Sylvia, connecting in 1988 after eight months of dating.

I must thank Floyd for his continuous love and support whenever our children had a crisis. In these crises, we could not play the blame game, because these circumstances resulted from both our traits.

You know, in marriages, people like to blame their spouses for certain situations that cause disagreement and pain. I want to encourage my married readers who have sick children to do all within your power to not blame your spouse or partner. We just need to be supportive and, most of all, continue to love each other.

God was with Floyd and me from the time we met, and all I can say is, despite our imperfections, He has done and continues to do great things in our lives.

CHAPTER 7
Gracious Children

When my children had a crisis, it would cause their red blood cells to get stuck while flowing in their chest, belly, or joints. Sometimes, this would totally block blood flow, depriving some body parts of the oxygen they needed. This, in turn, caused intense pain that could last from a few hours to a few weeks. That is why they spent so much time in the hospital. Whenever their pain became severe, we knew they would have to take pain medications for a minimum of ten days.

Most of their pain occurred in the arms, legs, chest, hands and feet, and even lower back. When I asked them,

"Where does it hurt?" they would tell me, "All over, Mom. All over." Other symptoms included breathing problems, extreme tiredness, headaches or dizziness, and even jaundice. I saw all of it happen to them.

Doctors always recommended that Vashti and Vance drink a lot of fluids so they would not get dehydrated. If they became dehydrated it was possible they could experience a sickle cell crisis and would need immediate medical treatment, including but not limited to spending time in the hospital. They loved to eat; however, I had to force them to eat their vegetables, which were essential for them to have. At school, they would have a doctor's certificate exempting them from any form of sports, due to their condition. However, they never wanted children to feel sorry for them, so if they felt good enough, they would participate in all sports and stop when they felt tired.

Heating pads or massages helped every time they had a crisis. If the pain got too severe— on a scale of 1 to 10, with 10 being the highest—we knew it was time to head to the hospital so they could get stronger pain medication or even have fluids directly injected into a vein.

At one point, doctors at Miami Children's Hospital put Vance on a new drug, hydroxyurea. This drug was supposed to help prevent abnormal red blood cells from forming, and Vance was asked to take this drug along with his regular folic acid. However, Vance had no love for this pink capsule that he was to take twice daily. When cleaning up his room, in Freeport and in Abaco, Floyd and I found most of the pink pills under his bed or under his pillow. He never took the medication as the doctor prescribed; although we had thought he was swallowing it, he was faking it.

Vashti was never placed on hydroxyurea, as her crises were fewer and further apart and she did not spend as much time in the hospital as a child as Vance did.

Even when in pain, the children would try their best to be gracious and polite. Floyd and I knew it was unintentional, but it felt as though the two of them had some sort of agreement about their crisis periods. When we finished dealing with one child, we would say to each other, "Look, the other one is jealous and looking for attention," because the following week, we would have to take care of the other. It felt as though they took turns at a game of some sort and when one said, "This week, I will be sick," the other would patiently always respond, "OK, but next week, it is my turn." Floyd and I, as parents, were seeing and treating the pain all the time—sleepless nights because of my girl with us in Abaco and phone calls about my son's episodes in Freeport.

When our children were together in the summertime or over holidays, they would sometimes say to us in the morning, "We did not wake you up, because we did not want to bother you," even though one of them had been up all night in pain. Whenever I would ask them why they did not call me, they would always say it was because they knew we had to sleep for work the next day. I would tell them how thoughtful they were to think about us when they knew that we were there to take care of them.

As they got older, they were both humble and always apologetic when in a crisis, worrying about having to go to the hospital yet again. I assured them that their father and I brought them into this world, and as they had inherited SCD from us, we had to take care of them. "You are our responsibility," I would say. "And do not hesitate to let us know when you are in pain," I repeatedly told them; but they usually waited until their pain became severe before they called us for help.

Every time I saw them in pain, it felt as if it were the first time, because it made me feel guilty all over again. I would ask myself why—why did I do this to such beautiful children? They would comfort me and say, "Mom, it's not your fault. Know that God will take care of us. You and Dad are always included in our prayers." This is when I realized that they had faith in God and were praying for a miracle to completely take away the disease.

To those other people who have sickle-cell disease, know that your parents, guardians, or caretakers feel your pain along with you. Do not take them for granted. They love you all the same and only ask that you have patience with them while they are serving you.

We parents, guardians, and caretakers need the strength to go into our children's rooms, see the pain on their cute faces, and put a smile on ours to keep them strong. As a parent of two children with the disease, I had double strength and would not trade my life experiences for anything, other than to do it again with love, love, and more love.

CHAPTER 8
Primary School

IN 1995, VASHTI STARTED SCHOOL AT COOPER'S TOWN Primary School, staying there until 2001, when she graduated at age eleven as head girl and valedictorian. She still enjoyed going to school so much that even when she went to the hospital, she insisted we bring her schoolwork with us so she would not fall behind.

She was always helpful at school and around the house as well. At school, she would be the teacher's handy girl, doing extra to help the other students. At home, she learned to cook, wash, and clean. She always told me that she was preparing for her life away from home.

She had some friends who were also our neighbours, and they became like my daughters. They took care of Vashti if Floyd and I had to work late. I think these friends learned to cook in my house because when we got home, we could smell the evidence, and yes, a pot of noodles or spaghetti with hot dogs was on the stove.

Those friends gave Vashti the nickname "Powie" because of her slim posture. In the Bahamas if you were very tall, skinny and underweight, we would call you "PO", however they added "WIE", pronounced po-we. They even took care of Vance whenever he would visit us from Grand Bahama, and he became like their brother. Floyd and I will forever be grateful to them, their family members, and the neighbours who looked out for her and also watched over our property.

As a child, Vance had hobbies that included playing video games, reading Japanese manga (comic books), and playing in the yard with his cousin, Stephon. He loved school so much that even when he was sick, he wanted to go; however, his grandmother would say that she wanted to nurse him and make him feel better, so he would just stay home. Also, during primary school, Vance joined the bird-watching club and could name almost fifty birds. He went on field trips with the club.

At school, Vance wanted to participate in all the regular physical education classes, which included basketball, soccer, and track and field. He was allowed to participate in all sporting activities, but if he felt tired, the coaches and teachers understood that a medical problem limited his abilities. Vashti remained with us in Abaco during her elementary years. Vashti was allowed to participate in all the regular physical education classes as well, and her coaches and teachers all had the same understanding about her disease. Neither of them wanted to be left out of any part of school, including school activities.

As I mentioned before, Vashti loved making friends. In primary school, Vashti had a friend named Shanadia who lived on another settlement, and she insisted that we consider taking Shanadia from her parents so she could live with us. Shanadia stayed with us from September 1999 to June 2001, when she and Vashti both graduated from the primary school in Cooper's Town, Abaco. Floyd and I call Shanadia our unofficial daughter, since we signed no official documents but she was a sister to Vashti and Vance. Shanadia now lives in a different country, where she is married and works for her husband's business.

In 2000, when Vashti was ten years old, she fell at school and had a severe pain, which we were told might be due to a swollen appendix, and if so, doctors would have to take it out immediately. We were advised to get a second opinion and were referred to Miami Children's Hospital in South Florida. Her condition was so severe that she had to be transported by air ambulance. When we arrived at Miami Children's Hospital, she had a series of doctor's visits and blood transfusions, and pain medications were administered to her. Ultimately, we realized the problem was not with her appendix. Instead, she had to be treated with antibiotics for ten days for fluid in her lungs.

CHAPTER 9
The Hurricane

I WILL NEVER FORGET WHEN VANCE GOT SEVERELY ILL AND had to be hospitalized at four years old. This crisis occurred in September 1999. The day we informed Dr Hunt of Vance's condition, he had suggested that we wait to see how he was in the morning, but because a hurricane was travelling towards Freeport, we needed to leave that night, before all flights would be grounded. We made arrangements and immediately flew to Miami Children's Hospital.

Can you guess the name of the hurricane? Floyd—the same name as Vance's dad. The Bahamas will never forget Hurricane Floyd, and we will not forget Hurricane Floyd for the rest of our lives.

We made it in time to Florida, and a few days later, we learned how much damage Hurricane Floyd had done to the Bahamas, in particular our home island, Abaco. It devastated us to learn that the hurricane had destroyed so many homes, but we thank God no lives were lost. Our home was safe as well, with the exception of a few shingles and a small piece of plywood from the roof.

The night before the hurricane was to hit South Florida, we visited Vance and stayed late into the night, but we had to return to the motel for our safety. The hurricane passed, and the following morning, we went to the hospital to see him. However, there was no Vance.

I almost lost my mind thinking he must have died and nobody had called to let us know. However, we discovered that because he was a patient on the hospital's critical list, staff had moved him and all other such patients to the hurricane shelter rooms in the hospital. This incident reminded me of how the

CIA would protect the president of the United States. In emergency situations, the CIA locked him away in a safe place, and only the good Lord could get to him. I was grateful that the hospital did that to protect my baby, but I knew God, whom I serve, was protecting him for us.

The staff took us somewhere in the hospital I had never gone in all the times I had been there before. And talk about protection—this place was like the White House! Vance had been well taken care of.

We had to stay in Florida for the next few weeks because of how severe his crisis had been. Daily, I went to the hospital chapel and prayed, "God, whatever is Your will, let it be done." Vance remained sedated for weeks, with only the ventilator for breathing and support. During this time, my husband and I got closer to God and closer as friends. We had only each other to talk to.

My family back home called us whenever they could, which was limited because of the devastation that Hurricane Floyd had caused in the Bahamas. I will never forget and will forever be grateful to Floyd's mom and my mom for their love and support. Also, my coworkers at that time, at the Royal Bank of Canada, really supported me and checked on me whenever time permitted them to do so.

Do not forsake family. Family is all we have, so we must love and support each other in times of crisis.

Miami Children's Hospital will go down in history as the hospital that provided the best care in the world during Hurricane Floyd. The hospital took care of Floyd and me and gave us peace of mind that our son was in the best care in the world—right next to the care of Jesus's hands, of course.

Hats off to the staff at Miami Children's Hospital.

CHAPTER 10
Trips to the Hospital

THE TRIPS TO MIAMI CHILDREN'S HOSPITAL FOR BLOOD transfusions started in 2000 (Vashti was ten then, and Vance was five). It concluded in 2003. (Vashti was age 13 and Vance age eight) My in-laws in Freeport were a great help during this time. Also, when Floyd and I couldn't take the children to Miami for their blood transfusion appointments, their aunt Evelyn Poitier was always able to take them for us.

Thank God for the boat named *The Discovery* that travelled between Fort Lauderdale and Freeport back in 2000. The kids travelled for half price, as they were under the age of twelve back then.

Floyd took pride in these trips because they gave him, as a father, time to bond with his children. Vance only required a one-day trip because his blood type was always ready for him. However, Vashti required a two-day trip because her blood had antibodies, so the hospital had to search for her match.

Vance and Vashti loved to go on these trips with Floyd because they always had their way and he would purchase whatever they had on their shopping list. I would say to him, "You spoil the children," but he would say, "Well, they are alive today and may be dead tomorrow, so please let them have fun while they can."

I will never forget the trip when I had to take Vance to Miami for his monthly transfusion and I also took Vashti along as a treat for being so good in school. While we were in the treatment room with Vance, she became ill and had to go to the emergency room. I said, "Lord, double for my trouble, one on the third floor and the other on the first floor."

This was the first time they were patients in the hospital at the same time. There alone, I prayed that the Lord would not let either of them be admitted for a long period. The Lord heard my prayers. Vance's blood transfusion was completed in a few hours. Vashti's stay in the emergency room also lasted only a few hours. I was able to leave with both of them. What a relief and a joy it was to see them feeling better and ready to travel. I withstood that test and came out stronger for the next.

Over this period, it was like a room in the hospital had their names on it. Everybody knew they were the family from the Bahamas. They used to get a toy from the playroom for every trip, so they received an unbelievable amount of toys from the hospital.

In addition to the toys they got from the hospital and the outpatient clinic, Vashti and Vance wanted even more toys from the famous Toys"R" Us store. We could not drive by without stopping. Even though we thought Vance could not see it, and we would only spell the store's name when we passed it, he would say, "I know you just passed my store." So, we had to turn around and go inside even if we had only just bought another teddy bear. His favourite thing to get was just some game cards, and hers was something from the Barbie doll collection.

No trip to Florida was complete without a visit to Toys"R" Us.

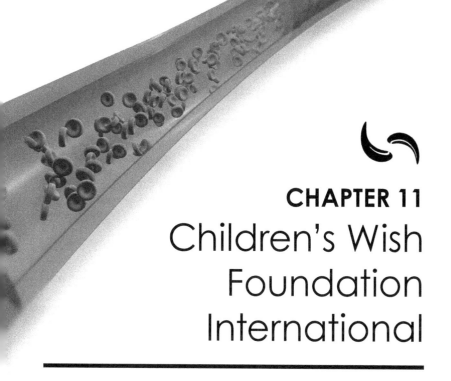

CHAPTER 11
Children's Wish Foundation International

In 2001, a social worker at Miami Children's Hospital asked me if we ever took vacations. I explained to her how difficult the past three years had been for us, as we had to bring the kids to Miami for their monthly blood transfusions.

By this time, the blood transfusions had actually started to get better, going from monthly down to every three months and then down to every six months. And we were told we would eventually need no more hospital visits for blood transfusions, as a new medication on the market could reduce blood transfusions. The name of the medication was Hydroxyurea but only it was prescribed to Vance because he had more sickle cell crisis than Vashti.

Anyhow, this sweet social worker then said that Children's Wish Foundation International (www. childrenswish.org) was now offering to grant wishes for people outside the United States and that she had placed our children's names on the list in hopes that they might be chosen to make a wish.

This really excited us, as we had only heard about the wish granting on TV and had thought it would never happen to us. In the end, Vashti and Vance were both chosen and were able to wish for whatever they wanted to do. Vance said he wanted to see snow, and Vashti wanted to see the Golden Gate Bridge in California. To our surprise and excitement, both trips were approved.

When Vance was seven and Vashti was twelve, we were given an all-expenses-paid one-week trip (plus spending money) for four to Niagara Falls over 21–27

January 2002. This vacation granted Vance's wish to see snow. This was truly our family's first real vacation with no doctor's appointments or hospitalizations and just completely stress-free time spent with our kids.

Despite our excitement about the trip, I feared how the cold would affect both our children and if they would develop a crisis while we were away. I was always checking what kind of weather to expect that week and advised their paediatrician of their whereabouts. He asked me not to worry and to even let the kids play in the snow but to just make sure that they wore their gloves, hats, boots, and thick jackets. So we made sure they were bundled up. All the tours that Children's Wish Foundation International scheduled for us were indoor activities, which made it easier for them to always stay warm.

Our second trip, which granted Vashti's wish, took us to San Francisco to see the Golden Gate Bridge. This was scheduled the following year, 10–16 March 2003, when Vashti was thirteen and Vance was eight. Vashti had always wanted to see the Golden Gate Bridge ever since she had read about it and seen it in magazines; but when she actually saw how amazing it looked in reality, I think it sparked her vision of becoming an engineer.

Children's Wish Foundation International also planned the tours for us there, so we just had to be ready in our hotel lobby each morning for the tour guides to pick us up and take us to the various spots.

We are so very grateful to the social worker from Miami Children's Hospital for thinking about us or feeling empathy for us. For the first time in a long time, we ended up having two good vacations as a family and enjoying trips away from home with no hospital visits.

CHAPTER 12
Vance's Trip to Camp Good Days

GARY MERVIS FOUNDED THE NONPROFIT ORGANIZATION Camp Good Days and Special Times Inc. (https://www.campgooddays.org) when his daughter Elizabeth "Teddi" Mervis was diagnosed with a malignant tumour at the age of nine. He saw how alone she felt at that time, being the only child in her school and neighbourhood dealing with cancer. With the help of many friends and community members in Greater Rochester, New York, the camp has provided Teddi and other children who have cancer with the opportunity to have residential camping experiences.

This camp—located in Branchport, New York, on the shore of Keuka Lake in the heart of the Finger Lakes Region—allows these children to come together with the only other ones who truly understand what they are going through.

Vance heard about the camp from Vashti, and Vashti had heard about it from her high school teacher, who knew that Vashti and her brother suffered from sickle-cell disease. Vance applied to the Bahamas Agent to go to the camp and was successful/

Joe Kohler, the Bahamas' regional representative for Camp Good Days and Special Times, is a long-time winter resident of the island of Grand Bahama. Mr. Kohler and a number of others, many from the Finger Lakes, have sponsored children from the tropical islands to attend Camp Good Days. Joe sponsored Vance and made it possible for him to attend the camp.

Vance made his first trip to Camp Good Days in the summer of 2008. The trip was an all-expenses-paid one, on which a teacher accompanied him from Walter Parker Primary School in Freeport, Grand Bahama. He made his second trip, during the summer of 2009, with his chaperone Dorothy Goldsmith; and he made the third and fourth trips with Dorothy and her husband, Terry Goldsmith. Terry Goldsmith was the program coordinator for the Family Islands.

In total, Vance was able to attend Camp Good Days every summer for four years. Even when Vance moved to Abaco, he still had the opportunity to travel with the Bahamas group that were camp attendees from Freeport. Each year, Vance would spend a few days before camp with Joe Kohler and his mom at their home in New York. He and Joe have been friends since 2008. During that time, Vance also became friends with the founders of Camp Good Days, Gary and Wendy Mervis.

Over the years, Camp Good Days has become one of the largest organizations of its kind, and still remains dedicated to improving the quality of life of children and families who have been touched by cancer and other life-threatening challenges. It offers these programs and services free of cost to participants.

As a beneficiary of these special times at Camp Good Days, Vance is truly grateful to the founders,

Gary and Wendy, to have gotten the opportunity to travel four years in a row, spend two-week periods with friends who also have sickle-cell disease, and form lifelong relationships and memories at Keuka Lake, New York.

Thank you so much, Camp Good Days, for touching my immediate and extended family with your generosity.

CHAPTER 13
Vashti—High School

EVEN THOUGH VANCE HAD MORE CRISES AS A BABY AND toddler, when Vashti got older and started her monthly cycle at age thirteen, we began to see her health decline with more frequent crises than before. As a young woman with a blood disorder, in addition to losing blood monthly as a result of menstruation, her crises became more painful for her. However, Vashti never complained and continued to give school her best shot.

From September 2001 to June 2004, Vashti attended secondary school at Long Bay School in Marsh Harbour, Abaco. In grade nine, she started doing technical drawing and drafting. She enjoyed that subject (and seeing the Golden Gate Bridge on vacation) so much that she decided to become an architect to be able to design her own house.

Vashti transferred to Jack Hayward High School to complete high school in Freeport, Grand Bahama, from September 2004 to June 2007. She was on the honour roll and graduated and got her diploma. She also received top awards in her drafting classes, and it made her conclude that it should definitely be her major at whatever college she chose.

She met many young ladies and men who became part of her group she called her *friends and associates*. I had to also make them part of my family because she was such a loving and caring person. Since there were too many to mention by name, I will just say thank you to all of you who made up Jack Hayward High's graduating class of 2007.

During high school, she was given the opportunity to participate in the school's job-training program. She chose to remain in her field of drafting and surveying and had the pleasure to work with Riviere and Associates Limited at both its locations, in Freeport and Abaco. Thanks to the staff who gave her this experience of a lifetime. She looked forward to those working days.

She lived with my sister, Izetta for one year and then completed her final years of high school while living with her other aunt, Queenie. This gave them both the opportunity to take care of her. My baby girl's move to Freeport was sad and happy at the same time. I wanted her to pursue her goals and aspirations so she could be happy.

Some people did not know why we let our children follow their dreams, but I knew in my heart this was best for Vashti. Some materials I read said that most children with sickle-cell disease do not live beyond age sixteen. So we wanted to make sure our children enjoyed the time that God allowed them on earth.

Imagine reading that your children's lives can stop at that age. It was not good at all, but I had to trust God—yes, trust God. I always encouraged myself to never give up on this challenge, for this was going to be a marathon and not a sprint.

CHAPTER 14
Vance—High School

At age eleven, Vance began his secondary education at Jack Hayward High School in Freeport, Grand Bahama. However, when the time came for his high school education, I told his grandmother that I wanted to relieve her as his caretaker and have him transfer to school in Abaco. I said it was time for him to bond with us at this age, so I was coming for my baby. As a grandmother, she said she was making the best decision for him. She had already enrolled him in high school, and she did not want to release him. My heart would not allow me to take him away from her because she said she would miss him so much. Vance stayed for two more years at high school in Freeport.

The discussion came up again, and after we did much deliberating and I almost begged her to let my son return to Abaco, Vance returned to our home. Ultimately, he left Freeport at age fourteen and relocated to Abaco to attend Sherlin C. Bootle High School in Cooper's Town, from where he graduated with his high school diploma in June 2012.

While in high school at Cooper's Town, Vance joined the Bahamas Maritime Cadet Corps and the debate team for extracurricular activities. When he was a member of the debate team, his high school participated in a local competition among other high schools in Abaco. The debate was called Model United Nations (MUN). His team won, which afforded them the opportunity to travel to New Providence and represent Abaco School District at a national competition. Vance's team won the national competition in 2011, for which the overall prize was an all-expenses-paid trip to represent the Bahamas at the Assembly of the United Nations in New York.

Vance was excited to travel and represent his high school and honoured to represent his country after graduation in 2012.

Upon completing his high school studies, at age seventeen, Vance had the privilege to travel to Holland College in Prince Edward Island, Canada. This was an all-expenses-paid trip with the Bahamas Maritime Cadet Corps for a few months of studies. However, after the third week, Vance experienced a sickle-cell crisis and was admitted to the hospital for a few days. Three days after being discharged, he had a second attack. But this time, the hospital on Prince Edward Island said it would not release him unless he decided to go to the Bahamas, a country whose warmer climate the doctors knew would improve his health. On the day he was released from the hospital, he was on a flight back home to the Bahamas.

I will always be grateful to the Bahamas Maritime Cadet Corps coordinators, as they made sure he was well enough to travel and even accompanied him to Nassau. Unfortunately, I said that must be the end of his studies in the maritime industry.

However, Vance did not give up, and at age

eighteen, he asked the Bahamas' maritime group coordinator to give him one more opportunity to get into the maritime industry. So, in 2013, Floyd and I agreed that he could do further studies at the Maritime Professional Training Center in Fort Lauderdale, Florida. On completing the courses, Vance applied for sea training with a local ship in Abaco. He completed the application, but when the doctor's report came back, he was denied entry because of his health issue. Vance said, "I will not let this stop me from getting a career in which I can work and take ownership of my disease."

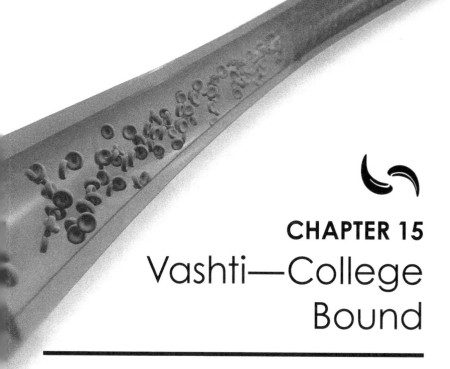

CHAPTER 15
Vashti—College Bound

In 2007, at age seventeen, Vashti started college prep at the University of the Bahamas, formerly the College of the Bahamas, in Nassau, Bahamas. She enrolled in August 2007, and in October of that same year, she had a crisis where she spent four days at Doctors Hospital. After one year at the University of the Bahamas, in August 2008, she was able to transfer the majority of her credits to Valencia Community College's West Campus in Orlando, Florida.

Vashti immediately adapted to her new environment; however, after about six months, she was in the hospital with a sickle-cell crisis. She endured the pain and said she was determined to graduate, taking her laptop with her in the hospital to do her homework. She completed her studies in December 2010 with two associate of arts degrees in land surveying and drafting. She also obtained additional certificates in advanced drafting and AutoCAD.

After she completed the associate of arts degrees, in 2011, I asked her if she wanted to take a break before continuing on with the bachelor's degree program. However, she said, "Mom, I can do it." She found the school she wanted to go to—Southern Polytechnic State University in Marietta, Georgia.

Vashti was determined that she would not let her sickness stop her from becoming what she wanted to be—the best female land surveyor in the Bahamas. In January 2011, she started a bachelor's degree program at Southern Polytechnic State University with an expected graduation year of 2014.

While in Marietta, Vashti had a few crises that took her to the emergency room. During these crises, she would call and say, "Mom, Dad, I am at the emergency room, but I am going to be OK. I just need them to hurry up and give me my pain medication so I can go home to prepare for school." I remember one evening she said she was going to the hospital and she was taking her laptop with her just in case the doctors told her she had to stay more than overnight. I told her to always keep a backpack for emergencies because sometimes she would be in so much pain that she would forget to pack her essentials.

Thankfully, Vashti's roommates made sure she was taken care of during those emergency days. She had some wonderful male and female friends and associates who supported her through the college years, and for this, our family from the Bahamas says thank you.

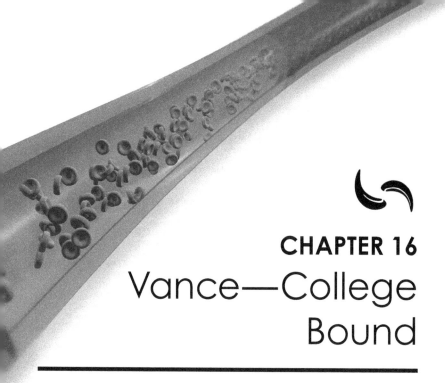

CHAPTER 16
Vance—College Bound

MY SON IS CURRENTLY ATTENDING THE SAME COLLEGE Vashti went to—Valencia Community College's West Campus—as I write this book.

Vance graduated from S. C. Bootle High School on 8 June 2012. Imagine losing your first baby on 20 May, eulogizing her on 2 June, and having your birthday on 7 June, all in the same year. That cannot be good for anyone, but look at me. I made it. When I think back now and see it was all in the Lord's will, I am able to encourage you, my readers, that you can also make it.

The family celebrated Vance's High School graduation with tears, as it comforted us to know that he made it through all those painful events. We gave God all the glory; but, at the same time, I questioned God. I asked Him what we, our family, had done to deserve this. I was reminded of Philippians 4:13, my favourite scripture: "I can do all things through Christ who strengthens me." This is where I found the strength of a lion to get up, brush myself off, and move on.

When Vance started applying to colleges, he had two choices—the University of Florida and Valencia Community College. His going to Valencia concerned me, as Vashti had gone there and he would have to deal with so many memories. He applied to both, and Valencia Community College accepted him first. He said, "See—that is where I'm destined to go." I agreed without hesitation because I knew Vashti would have approved of him following in her footsteps, as she had made her mark wherever she had gone. Although visits to Orlando have been sad at times, Vance always says that Vashti is looking down at us, wishing that we remain happy.

Vance decided that he would pursue computer science, and in August 2014, he made his way to Orlando to start at Valencia Community College. His quest for knowledge made him change his major a few years later. And he had three severe crises where he was in the hospital, and these set him back. He is determined to complete his studies and has said, "Mom, I can do it and will make you all proud to see me finish and finish strong."

CHAPTER 17
Vashti's Final Chapter

On Saturday, 12 May 2012, Vashti was admitted to the hospital for the usual crises to get treatment. The next day, Sunday, 13 May, was Mother's Day, and I went to church and cried all through the service. I prayed for healing. I did not tell my immediate family that Vashti was in the hospital because I thought she would get out in a few days, as usual.

When she called on Monday, 14 May, to say she was still there after three days and the pain was not reducing, I knew that it was time for me to go to her. I then informed immediate family members that I had to go to Atlanta right away because Vashti had been in the hospital for three days and her pain was not reducing. I arrived in Atlanta on Tuesday, 15 May, to be with her; however, she was discharged the next day. We visited the outpatient office on 17 May, and they said she could go back to school.

On the morning of Friday, 18 May, she said to me, "Mom, I will not register for summer classes. I think I want to come home and rest, to be fresh for the August 2012 semester." I told her whatever she wanted to do was fine with me.

Later that afternoon, she went online to cancel enrolment in her classes and left the funds that I had transferred for the summer classes in her account. When she woke up early on Saturday, she said, "Mom, I am not feeling well; take me to the hospital, please." We went to the hospital early that morning, and I was there all night with her.

I hurriedly left the hospital around 7 a.m. on Sunday, 20 May, to get her favourite breakfast—chicken noodles—and drove back to the hospital from her dorm as fast as possible (the normally fifteen-minute drive only took me ten, but at the time, it had seemed to take forever).

When I went to her room, I was told by the Nurse they had to move her to the critical care block of the hospital and that they would come get me when I could see her. I went to the cafeteria to wait.

After about fifteen minutes, while still in the cafeteria, I heard a call over the PA system: "Code blue! Code blue!" I knew from watching TV shows that this meant an emergency was happening in that room, such as cardiac or respiratory arrest. I remember thinking, *If that is Vashti's room, whatever is Your will, Lord, let it be done.*

A few minutes later, a nurse found me and asked, "Are you Vashti's mom?"

"Yes," I said.

She informed me that she had been looking for me and asked me to come with her. I asked her what had happened, and she responded, "The doctor needs to talk to you right away."

At that moment, a calm breeze came over me. I do

not know where it came from, but again, all I said was "Whatever is Your will, Lord, let it be done."

The nurse said that she needed to explain something to me. She took me to a room with a small window next to where Vashti was—from there, I could see Vashti lying on the bed, but I could not go in. The nurse said, "We have been trying to revive her, but there has been no response. Look at the doctors," she continued. "They will try to shock her for you to see that there is no response."

Just then, the doctors went on to do this three or four times so I could see that there was no response. I never thought I would be witness to a defibrillator in my lifetime, but yes, I witnessed them using it on my daughter.

At 1.43 p.m., the nurse with me said, "She has expired." The nurse then asked me whether I had any family members she could call to be with me. I informed her that I had come by myself from the Bahamas because my daughter was attending college in Marietta. I sat down for about ten minutes to get my composure before I called Floyd to let the family know that she had passed. I called two of her friends, one of them her roommate and the other a friend from Abaco living in Atlanta, to give them news of her death.

The nurse asked if I wanted the chaplain to come talk with me. I said yes. She questioned how I could be so calm and again asked me whether I was OK. I assured her that I would be fine and told her, "The Lord's will is done, and I cannot get upset."

The hospital chaplain came. She asked, "Where is the mom?"

"Here," I responded.

"You are the mom? And so calm?"

"I have the love of God, and there is a peace over me now because I know that she is resting," I said. The chaplain repeated she had never seen such calmness from a mother who had just lost her child. I assured her, saying, "I know the Lord, and I am OK."

Vashti Vernica Poitier died Sunday, 20 May 2012, at twenty-one years of age. God saw her struggles and said to her, "Come home. No more blood transfusions or pain medications; come rest with Me."

Vashti's death came with serious emotions and

questions from my family because she was always the stronger person and the one who encouraged me to never give up. I was—and continue to be—shattered, grief-stricken, and sorely diminished by her loss. In ways I had not thought possible, her passing tested and tried my faith. This magnified my trust in God and reaffirmed my faith.

As she was the joy of my youth and middle years, I had counted on Vashti to be my friend and comforter in my old age, even though she always said, "Mom, when you get old, I am putting you in a nursing home. You are getting grouchy as you get older." Now that she was gone, who would visit and care for me, even if I was not in a nursing home? Floyd and I always thought, as parents, that we would die before our children and thus have no need to prepare for the burial of a child.

After the years of pain Vashti and my family had gone through as a result of her disease and her struggle, I found heavenly solace amid the earthly loss. I believe with all my heart it was all God's plan to draw me closer to Him.

After speaking with a mortician from Freeport, who, in turn, spoke with a mortician in Atlanta, I was able to leave the hospital. That same night, to my surprise, my sister, Izetta, and my sister-in-law Mitchie flew in from the Bahamas to be with me. They made a sacrifice to travel that same day, and if I've never before said how much it meant to me, let me express my utmost gratitude to you both. Again, I thank God for family. I must again repeat the importance of treating family members with as much love and respect as you can—you never know when you'll need them and who will be there for you.

I spent the next few days in Marietta making arrangements with the funeral director and visit the University to let them know Vashti had passed away. The visit to the morgue to identify your child is so hard; I never imagined that I would have to do that at such an early age. Leaving the morgue and going back to her dorm ripped me apart.

Some of her friends came to her dorm. Most of them said they had no idea that she was a sickle-cell patient. I told them she never wanted anyone to feel sorry for her, so she mostly kept the pain to herself and they would have never known. She used to just smile it away.

As I was leaving Marietta and going to Freeport without my daughter, it really hit me that she was coming home on the plane not as a regular passenger but as cargo. She was now referred to as "the remains." I thought, *Lord, what is life? Only a vapour, yet we do not want to speak to each other. We want to get angry for small things. What is life? Life is coming home as cargo and not a passenger.*

Vashti arrived in Freeport, and we made funeral arrangements. The service was held on Saturday, 2 June 2012, at 11 a.m. at Freeport's Calvary Temple Assemblies of God Church.

I reminded myself that I needed to stay strong for Vance. I remained strong during the service; however, my worst time happened at the grave site, when Vashti's remains were being lowered into the ground, no more to be seen on this side of earth, but to be seen in glory.

The graveyard experience gave me an indescribable feeling of loss that only God can give you the strength to witness. I held on to my son when the casket was being lowered, telling him to never leave me. Yet, here I am today. I can leave him because of the peace of God that passeth all understanding, which has kept me to this day—the knowledge that God is in control and whatever He does is well done.

Vashti used to note her favourite quote, "Every obstacle presents an opportunity to improve our condition," at the bottom of all her emails, which she signed *Powie*.

Rest on, Vashti. Mom loves you, but Jesus loves you the best.

CONCLUSION

WRITING THIS BOOK HAS NOT BEEN EASY FOR ME, AS I seriously started this journal after the death of my daughter. However, I just want to use my experience to let others know that they can also get through what they're facing.

If you have a child who has a disease, do not give up. Know that God is in the picture, and do not let go of His hands. Life is a journey that helps us get to a place of healing. The journey of healing can be up, down, straight, and crooked, so if you have lost a child, may your journey be that of walking with God, and may you remain in His will.

I thought so many times about whether to even write this book. I had to get the strength to put it together. My son finally encouraged me to go ahead and write it. I asked him, "I can put anything about you in it and you will not be angry?"

"It will only be the truth," he responded. He continues to have faith in God and knows that God has kept him thus far. He also depends on God to take him through each day.

My son has been away from me since 2014, living on his own and going to college. He graduated from high school in June 2012, the same year Vashti died. He wanted to go to college immediately after high school graduation, but I could not let him go. I was afraid that he, like Vashti, would die in college.

Talk about your faith being tested! This was a test. I kept him close to me from June 2012 to August 2014. Ever since he left for college, I have daily struggled with the fear that something could happen to him and I am not there to protect him. After he left, I kept saying, "God, please release me from him. I put him in Your hands."

When he would call me from college, the first thought that would come to my mind was *He's sick, and I need to travel to see him.* I used to be so jumpy every time the phone rang that I was making myself sick without realizing it. My blood pressure would not stay normal, yet I kept saying, "God, I trust You." My doctor told me to continue to take my pills daily, or else she would have to give me a stronger dose.

I tried—God knows I tried—but after losing one child, I found it hard to let him go. Now, I can finally say, "God, he is in Your hands. Do whatever You want to do." I have no control over His plans, and only He knows His plans for my son.

Readers, it is not easy to let go of your children, even if they are alive. I had to come to terms with the fact that they are only given to us for a season, and some seasons we have no control over. *Trust God!*

Consider these words, lyrics from one of my favourite songs, the hymn "'Tis So Sweet to Trust in Jesus": "I'm so glad I learned to trust Thee, precious Jesus, Saviour, Friend. And I know that Thou art with me, wilt be with me to the end. Jesus, Jesus, how I trust Him! How I've proved Him over and over! Jesus, Jesus, precious Jesus! O for grace to trust Him more."

Trust God!

I wrote this book to encourage caretakers and parents of children with sickle-cell disease. I pray that it will indeed let you know that you are not alone and you can always reach out to me for support. Pain is no joke. Do not take it lightly; always act swiftly.

BIBLIOGRAPHY

KUNZ, JEFFREY R. M., ED., "BLOOD DISORDERS: SICKLE-Cell Anemia", in *The American Medical Association Family Medical Guide* (New York, 1982), 418–23.

ABOUT THE AUTHOR

ZETTA SYLVIA BAILLOU-POITIER WAS BORN 7 JUNE 1963 IN High Rock, Grand Bahama. She attended the all-age school in High Rock and graduated from Grand Bahama Catholic High School in 1979. She completed certification courses at Nassau Business Academy in 1980 and 1981.

She always wanted to become a stewardess because she loved to travel; however, she settled for studying business and remained in the field as a banker. For thirty-four years, she was employed as a banker with the Royal Bank of Canada in the Bahamas. The job afforded her opportunities to work as an administrator, loans officer, and collections officer. She retired in November 2015.

She is an active member of St. Andrew's Baptist Church of Fire Road, Abaco, Bahamas. She is also very active in numerous charity groups in Cooper's Town, Abaco, Bahamas

She comes from a small family of one sister and three brothers. Both her parents are alive and reside in High Rock, Grand Bahama, Bahamas.

She lives in Cooper's Town with her husband of thirty years, Floyd, and their son, Vance.